Rescue Crews

By Cameron Macintosh

Rescue crews can help us when we get lost.

They can help us if we are not well.

This rescue crew helps
if there is a blaze.

A few of the crew help
to put out the blaze.

This rescue crew helps us
if we are not well.

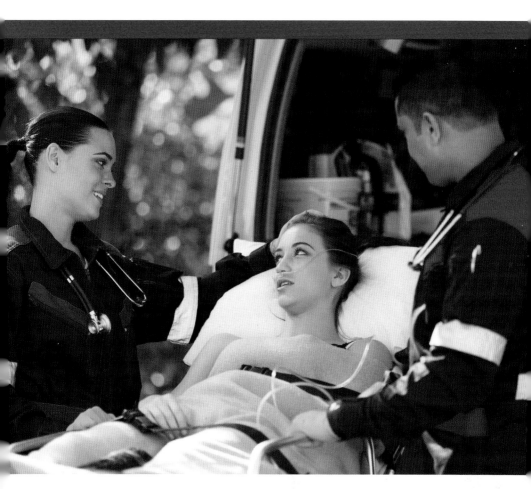

A big wind blew a tree
onto this home.

This rescue crew helps get
the tree off the home.

This rescue crew helps if
we get lost at sea.

They come and rescue us
in a boat.

This rescue crew helps us
if we get lost on land.

They can go up and down cliffs
to get to us.

This rescue crew flew
to pick up a sick man.

They lift him up and
get him home.

This rescue crew has dogs
that are good at sniffing!

The dogs can smell us
if we get lost.

Plus, they are cute!

This rescue dog is Hugo.

Hugo can dig us out
if we are stuck.

Rescue crews are the best!

We should value them a lot!

CHECKING FOR MEANING

1. How do rescue crews help people? *(Literal)*

2. How does Hugo know where to dig to find a lost person? *(Literal)*

3. What can we do to show how much we value rescue crews? *(Inferential)*

EXTENDING VOCABULARY

crews	What are *crews*? How do crew members work together to help other people? What is another word that means a group of people who work together? E.g. team.
cute	What does *cute* mean in this text? What other things do you know that can be described as cute?
value	What does *value* mean in this text? What other words have a similar meaning? E.g. respect, appreciate. What do you value?

MOVING BEYOND THE TEXT

1. Name some jobs people do where they might rescue people. E.g firefighters, police officers, paramedics.

2. Discuss the photo on page 2. What is happening in this picture?

3. What different types of transport do rescue workers use? Why?

4. Talk about other jobs that working dogs do. What special training do they need?

SPELLINGS FOR THE LONG /u/ VOWEL SOUND

u	ue	ew	u_e

PRACTICE WORDS

crews

rescue

few

crew

blew

cute

Hugo

flew

value

Rescue